At the Edge
of the Sea

Written by Ann Goodale

The Splash Zone

Have you ever walked along a beach and seen where the ocean meets the land? It is fun to wade along the edge of the sea and look at the things washed up on the beach. The edge where the sea touches the land is known as the **splash zone**. In some places, the splash zone is shallow, with sand under the water.

In other places, the splash zone is rocky. Look at the seaweed floating among the rocks in this photo. This seaweed is called **kelp**.

Tide pools at the edge of the sea
can be exciting.
Little fish swim around.
Crabs hide in the seaweed.

If you pick something up from the beach, take care. It could still
be alive. You wouldn't want to damage it.

Sea Urchins

Some sea creatures are poisonous and can be dangerous.
Sea urchins are covered with poisonous spines.
Usually, when you find sea urchins on the beach, the spines have worn off, and they are safe to pick up.

The sea urchin on the right is still covered with spines.
The sea urchin on the left is safe to pick up.

Octopuses

A small octopus is easy to see
in shallow water.
An octopus can spit out a cloud
of purple-black ink to defend itself.

An octopus can squirt water as well as ink.

One small octopus is very dangerous.
It is called the **blue-ringed octopus**.
People who touch this octopus can die.
Sometimes blue-ringed octopuses
will hide in shells or empty drink cans.
Never, ever touch one.

A blue-ringed octopus

Shells

Shells, shells, and more shells.
It is nice to pick up different shells
along the beach.
They once had sea animals
living inside them.

Did you know?

A shell that is joined in two halves is called a **bivalve**.

Cone shells are shaped
like ice-cream cones.
Some animals living in cone shells
have poisonous stings.
If there is a live animal inside,
don't pick up the shell.
Only pick up shells that are empty.

A cone shell

Crabs

When a shell is empty, it can be
useful to other creatures living
at the edge of the sea. Empty shells
often become homes for crabs.
Hermit crabs have to choose
bigger and bigger shells as they grow.
Most crabs don't need to live
inside other shells.
Their own shell, or **carapace**,
is tough enough to protect them.

A hermit crab inside a borrowed shell

Sea Anemones

Sea anemones are often very colorful. When they open up, they look like flowers, but they are really animals. Anemones have stinging capsules. They are related to jellyfish and coral.

Cherry anemones

Starfish

Starfish (or sea stars) are often brightly colored when they are alive under the water. They lose their bright colors when they die. Did you know that a starfish has its mouth underneath it, in its middle? It sucks food into its stomach through its mouth.

Starfish are often easy to find.

Sea Slugs

If you wade quietly and watch carefully, you might see some interesting sea creatures. A tiny sea slug might swim by, for example.

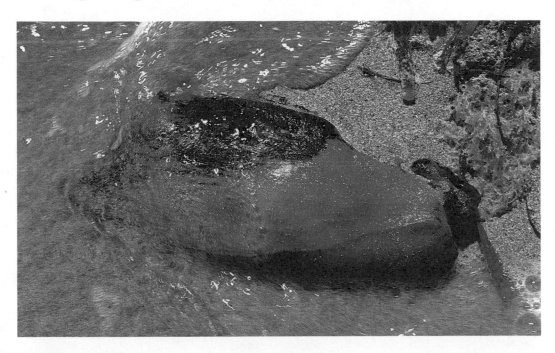

A sea slug

Some larger sea slugs can't swim. They crawl on the bottom of the sea. We might see them when they crawl onto the beach to die.

Sea Birds

When you go to the beach, see how many different types of sea birds you can find.

This is a fairy tern chick. It is trying to hide in its shallow nest right on the beach.

An oystercatcher looks for food.

A Pacific gull scavenges for scraps left on the beach.

Pelicans enjoy wading in the shallow water.

A brown booby keeps guard over her chick.

Turtles

Turtles sometimes come onto a beach at night to lay eggs.
Later, the young turtles hatch and struggle back down the beach to the water.

The female turtles leave large tracks on the beach as they go up to dig big holes and lay their eggs.

A green turtle digs a hole for its eggs.

This green turtle is laying eggs.

A baby turtle heads for the water.

Seals and Sea Lions

Seals are very good swimmers
and spend a lot of time in the sea.
But they come back to land
to give birth to their young.

This fur seal looks as though it owns the beach.

Sea lions are a special type of seal.
Sea lions can be very fierce.
It is wise to leave them alone.
Seals and sea lions have four flippers
that help them swim well in the sea.
Sea lions and some other seals can use
their flippers to walk on land, too.

A group of sea lions rests at the edge of the sea.

Dolphins

In some places, friendly dolphins will come close to the beach.

Did you know that dolphins are a special kind of whale?

Reefs

Look at this picture of a rocky reef.
The reef is covered with shallow water.
At the edge of the reef, the water
is deeper and light green.
Where the water becomes
dark blue, it is very deep.

In warm parts of the world, beautiful coral grows along reefs in shallow water near the edge of the sea.

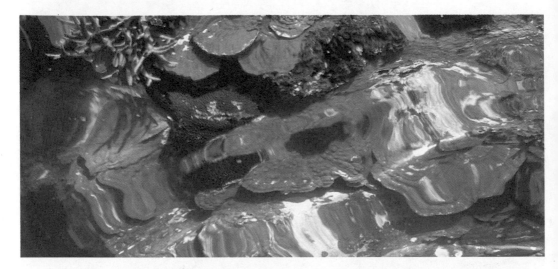

Some coral is brightly colored.

This soft coral doesn't look so colorful.

At the Beach

Next time you are near a beach,
look to see if anyone
has left litter lying around.
Many pieces of plastic or other litter
can harm sea creatures.
We need to protect our beaches
and our wildlife.

INDEX